CHILDREN'S ENCYCLOPEDIA

THE WORLD OF KNOWLEDGE

INVENTIONS AND DISCOVERIES

Manasvi Vohra

V&S PUBLISHERS

Published by:

V&S PUBLISHERS

F-2/16, Ansari road, Daryaganj, New Delhi-110002
☎ 23240026, 23240027 • *Fax:* 011-23240028
Email: info@vspublishers.com • *Website:* www.vspublishers.com

Regional Office : Hyderabad
5-1-707/1, Brij Bhawan (Beside Central Bank of India Lane)
Bank Street, Koti, Hyderabad - 500 095
☎ 040-24737290
E-mail: vspublishershyd@gmail.com

Branch Office : Mumbai
Jaywant Industrial Estate, 1st Floor–108, Tardeo Road
Opposite Sobo Central Mall, Mumbai – 400 034
☎ 022-23510736
E-mail: vspublishersmum@gmail.com

Follow us on:

PUBLISHER'S NOTE

V&S Publishers is glad to announce the launch of a unique, set of 12 books under the head, *Children's Encyclopedia – The World of Knowledge.* The set of 12 books namely – *Physices, Chemistry, Space Science, General Sceince, Life Science, Human Body, Electronics & Communications, Scientists, Inventions & Discoveries, Transportation, The Earth, and GK (General Knowledge)* has been especially developed keeping in mind the students and children of all age groups, particularly from 6 to 14 years of age. Our main aim is to arouse the interest and solve the queries of the school children regarding the various and diverse topics of Science and help them master the subject thoroughly.

In the book, *Inventions and Discoveries,* the author has broadly dealt with some world popular Inventions & Discoveries like *Bacteria, Vitamins, Rabies Vaccine, Penicillin, Aeroplane, Electricity, Cinema, Electric Bulb,* and so on...

Each chapter is followed by a section called **Quick Facts** that contains a set of interesting and fascinating facts about the topics already discussed in the chapter. At the end of the book there is **Glossary** of difficult words and scientific terms to make the book complete and comprehensive.

Quick Facts

- Galileo Galilei taught geometry, mechanics and astronomy at the University of Padua from 1592 to 1610.

Though our aim is to be flawless, but errors might have crept in inadvertently. So we request our esteemed readers to read the book thoroughly and offer valuable suggestions wherever necessary to improve and enhance the quality of the book. Hope it interests you all and serves its purpose well.

CONTENTS

Inventions & Discoveries

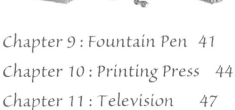

INVENTIONS AND DISCOVERIES

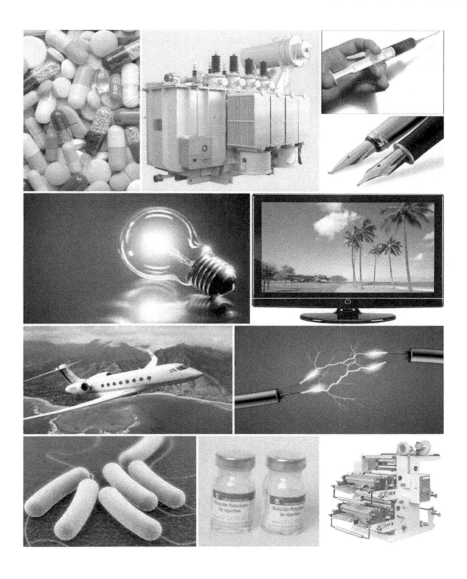

Chapter - 1

BACTERIA

Bacteria are one of the *micro-organisms* to populate the planet, earth. Mostly a few micrometres in size, bacteria are found in many different shapes like spheres, rods, spirals, etc. Bacteria are about *1000 nanometres in size*. (A nanometre is one-millionth of a millimetre).

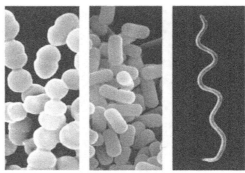
Bacteria of Different Shpaes

They are present in most of the habitats on the earth, in every climate and region. They are found in soil, water, air and even inside the earth's crust. They are also found in organic matter and on the bodies of other living organisms.

Did You Know?

There are around 40 million bacteria in a gram of soil and around one million in a millimetre of freshwater.

Antonie Van Leeuwenhoek

Bacteria were first found by Antonie Van Leeuwenhoek in the year, 1667 with the help of a single lens microscope. He was the first microbiologist in the history of science and he made this discovery using the microscope of his own design. He named the micro-organisms 'animalcules'. Later, he published his discovery in the Letters to the Royal Society.

Antonie Van Leeuwenhoek

Did You Know?

The name, **bacterium** was coined by **Christian Gottfried Ehrenberg** in **1828**.

Single-celled bacteria were the first form of life to appear on planet earth around four million years back. They are an important part of the earth's evolution. They help in many natural processes like secreting enzymes for natural decay, recycling nutrients, dissolving complex compounds, etc.

Ehrenberg

There are millions of bacteria in a human body. Some are made ineffectual by the immune system of the body, some are good for human health, while some are infection causing too. Certain bacteria found in things like curd, yeast, etc are good for the human digestive system. But some bacteria cause life threatening diseases like cholera, anthrax, diarrhoea.

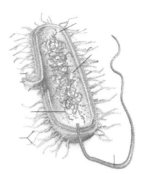
A Bacterial Cell

Quick Facts

- 💡 **The study of bacteria is known as Bacteriology. It is a branch of Microbiology.**
- 💡 **Different bacteria can live at a huge range of temperatures, from ice or snow to hot springs, and can even live in radioactive waste.**

- Most bacteria are useful – gut bacteria produce vitamins that help human beings and animals digest their food, and bacteria in the roots help legumes (plants in the pea and bean family) get nitrogen out of the soil, which helps them to grow.

- Bacteria are used in making cheese, yoghurt and sourdough bread.

- Bacteria produce oxygen – perhaps as much as half of the oxygen in the atmosphere.

- Bacteria (usually dead or weak ones) are used to make vaccines.

- Bacteria are used to clean water in sewage plants.

- Bacteria can cause food poisoning (sickness and diarrhoea) - this is why chicken needs to be cooked thoroughly, and why some food should be kept in the fridge.

- Bacterial infections can be cured with antibiotics – drugs that kill bacteria.

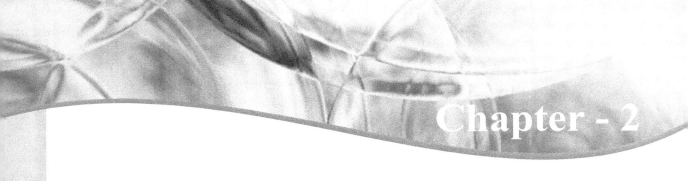

Chapter - 2

VITAMINS

A vitamin is an organic compound. It is an important nutrient required in an organism for living healthily. The word, vitamin is derived from 'vitamine' by Polish scientist Casimir Funk. Vitamine was a combination word made up of words-- vital and amine.

In other words, a vitamin is an organic compound which cannot be produced in the human body and is derived from other sources like vegetables, fruits, sunlight, milk, etc. Vitamins are needed in a very small amount for the human body. Lack of necessary vitamins cause certain defects and weaknesses in human beings.

Vitamin K1

There are a number of different types of vitamins which have different functions to promote health. They are vitamin **A, B1, B2, B3, B5, B6, B7, B9, B12, C, D, E** and **K**. Some vitamins act to control the metabolism rate, some regulate the growth of the body, and some help in maintaining the immune system, etc.

Until 1930, the only source of vitamins was food intake. Since then, vitamins have been extracted from their natural sources and sold as food supplement tablets at very cheap rates.

Frederick Gowland Hopkins

Frederick Gowland Hopkins or Sir F. G. Hopkins is known as the 'Father of British Biochemistry'. He was the one who firmly established the existence of vitamins in certain food items. He observed that there was something more than proteins, carbohydrates, minerals and fats in a balanced diet of food which keeps the body healthy. This, he and other scientist concluded, were altogether different nutrients required for maintenance of a living organism.

F.G. Hopkins was knighted in the year, 1925 as Sir F. G. Hopkins and in 1929, he shared the Nobel Prize in Physiology and Medicine with Christiaan Ejikman for their discovery of growth stimulating vitamins.

Did You Know?

Intake of Vitamin C helps in strengthening immunity and helps in reducing the effects of cough and common cold. Citrus fruits are the best natural sources of Vitamin C.

It is a fact that consumption of vitamins that exceeds from what is required can cause overdose and side effects and it is also true that deficiency of vitamins from what is required causes diseases and medical ailments. So below is a list of top ten essential vitamins with their sources and deficiencies, overdose and side effects. Knowledge of all these will help you determine which food sources provide which types of vitamins and deficiency, and overdose of which vitamins cause what type of medical diseases. This simple but complete guide of top ten vitamins will help you in building a healthy and balanced diet, which will be full of nutrition.

Food Sources of Vitamin A

Meat, eggs, cheese, milk, cream, kidney, liver and cod liver oil, all these, except for skimmed milk are high in saturated fat and cholesterol and are sources of Vitamin A. Carrots are a rich source of Vitamin A, in vegetables.

Milk

Egg

Meat

Deficiencies, Overdose, And Side Effects of Vitamin A

Vitamin A deficiency can cause vision problems and increase susceptibility to infectious diseases. Vitamin A overdose can cause birth defects. Acute vitamin A poisoning can occur when an adult takes several hundred thousand units of vitamin A supplements per day.

Food Sources of Vitamin B12

Beef, poultry, eggs, seafood and milk and its derivatives contain Vitamin B12.

Vitamin B12 deficiency occurs when the body is unable to absorb it from the intestinal tract, which may be caused due to pernicious anaemia (decreased red blood cells). Lower levels of Vitamin B12 can cause anaemia, numbness or tingling in the arms and legs along with weakness and loss of balance.

Poultry (Hen)

Milk

Eggs

Food Sources of Vitamin B6

Nuts, beans, legumes, meat, eggs, fish, enriched breads, cereals and whole grains are some sources of Vitamin B6.

Deficiencies, Side Effects and Overdose of Vitamin B6

Vitamin B6 overdose can cause neurological disorders, weakness, and numbness. Vitamin B6 deficiency can cause ulcers of the mouth and tongue, irritability, confusion, anxiety and depression.

Food Sources of Vitamin B1

Cereals, breads, pasta, lean meats (especially pork), fish, whole grains (especially wheat germ) dry beans, soybean, and peas contain vitamin B1.

Breads and Buns

Cereals (Whole Grains)

Fish

Vitamin B1 Deficiency

Deficiency of Vitamin B1 can cause fatigue, weakness, nerve damage, and psychosis. Excessive consumption of alcohol impairs absorption of this vitamin, which can lead to the development of a disease called beriberi (may affect cardiovascular or nervous system).

Food Sources of Vitamin B3

Poultry, dairy, fish, nuts, lean meat, and eggs contain vitamin B3. Cereals also supply some of this vitamin.

Egg	*Red Meat*	*Fish*	*Dairy Products*	*Hen (Chicken)*	*Nuts*

Deficiencies, Side Effects and Overdose of Vitamin B6

Vitamin B6 deficiency causes pellagra and the symptoms of pellagra include inflammation of the skin, mental deterioration and digestive

problems. Vitamin B6 overdose can cause peptic ulcer disease, liver damage and skin rash. Even normal doses can be associated with the reddening of the skin.

Food Sources of Biotin

Fish, eggs, dairy products including milk, curd, butter, legumes, whole grains, broccoli yeast, some vegetables in the cabbage family, sweet potatoes, and lean meat contain biotin.

| Butter | Curd | Legumes and Nuts | Milk | Food Grains |

Overdose of Biotin

Biotin or Pantothenic acid overdose produces symptoms of possible diarrhoea.

Food Sources of Vitamin C

Citrus fruits and juices, tomatoes, strawberries, broccoli, sweet potatoes, papaya, cantaloupe, cauliflower, Brussels sprouts, cabbage, raspberries, blueberries, and pineapple contain vitamin C. Also one citrus orange contains 45 mg of Vitamin C.

| Citrus Fruits | Tomatoes | Strawberries | Broccoli | Sweet Potatoes |

Vitamin C Overdose and Side Effects

Amounts exceeding 2,000 mg/day of vitamin C supplements can lead to stomach upset and diarrhoea. A small amount can cause inflammation and bleeding of the gums, rough and dry skin, decreased rate of wound healing and so on.

Food Sources of Vitamin D

Fish, dairy products, fortified cereals, oysters and margarine are some Vitamin D rich foods.

Fish   *Dairy Products*   *Fortified Cereals*   *Oysters*

Deficiencies, Overdose and Side Effects of Vitamin D

Vitamin D deficiency causes osteoporosis in old people and rickets in children. Vitamin D overdose causes undesirable effect that starts removing calcium from the bones and place them into other vital organs like heart and lungs, thereby reducing their overall capacity and function. Therefore, the inability to use heart and lungs properly can cause rickets.

Food Sources of Vitamin E

Corn, wheat germ, seeds, nuts, spinach, olives, vegetable oils, asparagus, sunflower, corn, soybean, and cottonseed contain high levels of Vitamin E.

Corn   *Wheat Germ*   *Seeds & Nuts*   *Spinach*   *Olives*   *Vegetable Oils*

Deficiencies, Side Effects and Overdose of Vitamin E

Vitamin E overdose at 400 International Units per day or more than that may increase the risk of death, but consuming multivitamins, which contain Vitamin E, is not harmful because of lose dose and quantity of vitamin E in the multivitamin supplements.

Food Sources of Vitamin K

Cauliflower   *Cabbage*   *Corn*   *Spinach*   *Soybeans*   *Vegetables*

Cauliflower, cabbage, corn, spinach, soybeans and other green vegetables contain Vitamin K. Vitamin K is absorbed by the bacteria that lines the gastrointestinal tract.

Vitamin K Deficiency

Deficiency of Vitamin K is very rare but it occurs when our body is unable to absorb vitamin K from the intestinal tract, which increases the chances of bleeding and bruising and uncontrolled bleeding because of the stoppage of normal clotting system which is essential for the regularisation of the blood system.

Least but not last, it should be noted that only overdose of vitamins can cause side effects, but then also before taking these vitamins and to know the recommended dosages, you should consult with your family physician, dietician, or doctor of naturopathy.

Quick Facts

- **Metabolism is the process of digesting the consumed food and deriving the required nutrients from it.**
- **A vitamin is an organic compound required as a nutrient in tiny amounts by an organism.**
- **Vitamin A was given the first letter of the alphabet, as it was the first to be discovered.**

- Vitamins are classified as either water-soluble or fat-soluble. In humans, there are 13 vitamins: 4 fat-soluble (A, D, E and K) and 9 water-soluble (8 B vitamins and vitamin C).

- Vitamin C helps to slow down or prevent cell damage. Vitamin C is an antioxidant but is also vital for the production of collagen and enhances iron absorption.

- Vitamin E is a powerful antioxidant, neutralizing cell-damaging free radical in the body.

- Vitamin E also protects the skin from the harmful effects of ultraviolet light.

- It has been proven that cancer is a deficiency disease caused by the lack of Vitamin B17 (Laetrile).

Chapter - 3

RABIES VACCINE

Rabies vaccine, as the name suggests, is a vaccination used to prevent and control rabies disease in humans and animals.

Rabies-The Disease

Rabies is an infectious disease caused by *rabies virus*. The rabies virus is a RNA virus which affects the *brain and the spinal cord*, in short the central nervous system, of humans as well as of animals. The virus travels from nerve cells to the brain of the mammal. On reaching the brain, it multiplies in

Rabies Vaccine

number and causes destruction of brain cells which causes death. The infection might become deadly if not treated well before the symptoms appear.

Structure of the Rabies Virus

The rabies viruses generally attack animals like *dogs, bats, skunks, foxes*, etc. It is through these animals that the disease gets spread

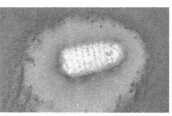
Rabies Virus

in *human beings*. As it is a communicable disease, the rabies virus spread through animal saliva or brain tissues. Mostly, it gets transmitted to human beings through dog bite. Rabies virus attacks the nervous system and the person starts having hallucinations, agitation, seizures, then finally coma and death. In animals, the symptoms usually are irritation, agitation and aggressive behaviour.

Louis Pasteur and Emile Roux

Louis Pasteur

Emile Roux

Prior to the discovery of the rabies vaccine, every rabid-case would result in death. In 1888, two French scientists, **Louis Pasteur** and **Emile Roux** developed the first rabies vaccine. Pasteur, unlike his many colleagues, did not follow the theory that 'diseases come from nowhere'. His main focus of work was to determine the causes behind various diseases.

Did You Know?

The rabies vaccine was first used on a *nine-year-old Joseph Meister on July 6, 1885*, who had been bitten by a rabid dog. *He was the first human being to be vaccinated by rabies vaccine.*

The Cure of Rabies

The rabies vaccine was made up of a sample of virus cultivated from infected and dead rabbit. The sample was weakened by allowing it to dry for a few days.

Pasteur observed that while transmitting rabies virus from one rabbit to another, the healthy rabbit did not become as sick as the first one. This meant that the rabies virus was weakening and injecting the healthy rabbit with the weak virus which gave immunity to the healthy rabbit.

- Rabies occurs everywhere and kills at least 55,000 people per year.

- The rabies virus was not seen through a microscope until 1950s.

- Most human cases of rabies are due to transmission of the virus through dog bites. Other animals that can carry the rabies virus include cats, raccoons, skunks, bats and livestock.

- Early symptoms of rabies in humans are similar to flu, with fever and fatigue. The rabies virus then damages the central nervous and respiratory systems. The final stages may include paralysis or hyperactivity and then coma and death.

- If you are exposed to rabies, the wound or exposure site should be cleaned and disinfected immediately. An anti-rabies vaccine must also be administered as soon as possible.

- Once the symptoms of rabies appear in humans, no treatment is possible, and the infected person almost always dies within a week.

Chapter - 4

PENICILLIN

Introduction

Penicillin is the world's one of the first antibiotic to be discovered. It is derived from a mold called penicillium. Discovery of penicillin pioneered a historic start in the field of antibiotics.

Penicillin Capsules

Before the discovery of penicillin, there were no cures for diseases like *pneumonia, gonorrhea, rheumatic fever*, etc. Antibiotics are compounds produced by *bacteria, fungi* and other *microscopic species* to counterattack other species.

Did You Know?

The development of penicillin has been regarded as an International Historical Chemical Landmark by *The American Chemical Society* and the *Royal Society of Chemistry*, on *November 19, 1999*.

Alexander Fleming

Alexander Fleming was a *Professor of Bacteriology* at *St. Mary's Hospital in London*. He discovered **Penicillin** in **1928**.

As a professor of bacteriology, Fleming studied different types of bacteria. Once, he was studying some bacteria which cause sore throats, boils, etc. He found that in one dish there is a blob of mold. Studying it further, he found out that mold secreted some kind of

Alexander Fleming

substance which killed the bacteria surrounding it. Thus, he observed that mold had some kind of substance which reduces the growth of infection causing bacteria.

Howard Florey

Later, penicillium research shifted to Oxford University. In 1940, Howard Florey, a scientist at Sir William Dunn School of Pathology, observed that penicillin can protect mice from a death-causing bacteria infection.

However, this research yet couldn't be used for mass welfare as it needed a large quantity of this mold culture. Florey, along with Norman Heatley, came to US with a small amount of penicillin, during the war days.

Production of Penicillin

A process of producing large quantity of penicillium mold was found out. Air was pumped into deep vats of corn steep liquour (a byproduct of milling process). To this, other key ingredients were mixed which resulted in faster growth of penicillin in a large amount.

However, it was a small amount of penicillin found in a moldy cantaloupe in a Peoria market which was used for mass production of the antibiotic.

- Antibiotics are natural substances released by bacteria and fungi to safeguard themselves.
- Bacteriology is the study of bacteria.

Some of the side effects of Penicillin are:

- Diarrhoea that is watery or bloody.
- Fever, chills, body aches, flu symptoms.
- Easy bruising or bleeding, unusual weakness.
- Urinating less than usual or not at all.
- Severe skin rashes, itching, or peeling.
- Agitation, confusion, unusual thoughts or behaviour.
- Seizure (black-outs or convulsions).

Chapter - 5

AEROPLANE

Introduction

Aeroplane or Airplane is the *fastest means of transportation* commercially today.

Prior to airplanes, air travel was limited to gliders, hot air balloons, etc. But these were not successful commercially.

Since the advent of the air travel, many attempts have been made for manufacturing an efficient and affordable means of air transportation. With the invention of a power propelled aircraft, the commercial scope of air travel has been met efficiently.

An Aeroplane

The Wright Brothers

In the year, **1903**, Wright brothers, **Orville and Wilbur** demonstrated the first ever airplane with a propeller. It was the first aircraft carrying a man, propelled by a machine which flew by its own power at an even speed and descended down without any damage. In the commercial sense, it was the basic design of an aircraft which would change the course of high speed transportation in the modern world.

The Wright brothers started with building and testing gliders. In the year 1900, they tested their new biplane glider weighing 50 pounds. Next year, they flew the largest glider ever but this one also faced problems. They conducted some tests and based on them, Wright brothers thought of building powered aircraft.

Wright Brothers

Their first airplane was named 'Flyer' which had a 12 horse powered engine.

After this airplane invention of Wright brothers, inventors started improving on these models and soon the world saw the advent of jet planes.

Working of an Aeroplane

A Jet Plane

An airplane flies on the basis of four things – thrust, drag, weight and lift. A propeller helps the plane to move forward with a high speed. This is called thrust. But the air in the atmosphere opposes the speed of the plane. This is called the drag. Thus, in order to move forward, thrust must be greater than drag. Now, to move upwards in the sky, the plane needs to have a lift which can overcome the barrier of the plane's weight. For this purpose, wings are used. Airplane wings are curved from top and linear from below. Thus, air moves faster on top of the wing and slower below. This lifts the plane up in the air. The wings help in changing the direction of the plane by rolling on either side. By lifting up the nose, the pitch of the plane can be raised.

- The pitch of the plane means to climb up or descend down.

- The first United States coast to coast airplane flight occurred in 1911 and took 49 days.

- An airplane's "blackbox" is a device which records conditions and events on an air vessel. A "blackbox" is actually orange in color to make it more visible in the wreckage. The term black box might come from its charred appearance after an air crash.

- A 747-400 has six million parts (half of which are fasteners) made in 33 different countries.

- The outer skin of an aeroplane is only 5 mm thick. During takeoff, when full of high pressure air, the take-off weight is increased by about a ton.

Chapter - 6

ELECTRICITY

Electricity has fast become one of the basic needs today, along with air, water, food and shelter. It is a form of energy which is used to run appliances, devices, gadgets, machines, etc – from the most basic ones to the advanced machines.

What is Electricity?

Electricity, in scientific terms, is the *flow of electrons*. When there is a continuous flow of electrons through a conductor like metal wire, then it is known as current. This current, in simple terms, is also known as electricity.

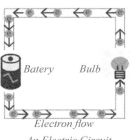

Electron flow
An Electric Circuit

You can produce electric charge by rubbing one end of your ruler with wool. Rub it continuously for a few minutes. Then bring it near a piece of paper. You'll notice that the piece of paper would cling to the ruler. This shows that an electric charge has been developed at the end of the ruler, which is attracting the paper.

Benjamin Franklin

Benjamin Franklin was a *physicist* who is credited for discovering electricity. He is known for his famous kite experiment during which he observed that lightning is electricity. In June **1752**, he attached a metal key to the string of a kite and flew it in a rainy sky. He noticed that there were some sparks jumping towards his hand from the metal key. He deduced that after getting wet, the string became a good conductor and through this string, the electric charges in the atmosphere travelled to the metal key in the form of sparks.

Benjamin Franklin

Did You Know?

Lightning is the most dramatic effect of electricity.

This was a breakthrough. Franklin's experiment proposed the basic principles of electricity.

Later, these principles were applied in various fields of physics like electromagnetism. Many great scientists based their research on these principles and invented the electric motor, electric bulb and many more electric run devices.

Lightning

How is Electricity Produced?

The most basic device for producing electricity is a **generator**. Put a coil of copper wire between the poles of a magnet. Attach the copper wire ends to a shaft. On rotating the shaft, the copper wire coil would also rotate within the magnetic field. This produces electric current or electricity.

Electricity is the science, engineering, technology and physical phenomena associated with the presence and flow of electric charges. Electricity gives a wide variety of well-known electrical effects, such as lightning, static electricity, electromagnetic induction and the flow of electrical current in an electrical wire. In addition, electricity permits the creation and reception of electromagnetic radiation such as radio waves.

In electricity, charges produce electromagnetic fields which act on other charges. Electricity occurs due to several types of physics:

- Electric charge: a property of some subatomic particles, which determines their electromagnetic interactions. Electrically charged matter is influenced by, and produces, electromagnetic fields.

- Electric current: a movement or flow of electrically charged particles, typically measured in amperes.

- Electric field: An especially simple type of electromagnetic field produced by an electric charge even when it is not moving (i.e., there is no electric current).

The electric field produces a force on other charges in its vicinity. Moving charges additionally produce a magnetic field.

- Electric potential: The capacity of an electric field to do work on an electric charge, typically measured in volts.

- Electromagnets: Electrical currents generate magnetic fields, and changing magnetic fields generate electrical currents.

In electrical engineering, electricity is used for:

- Electric power (which can refer imprecisely to a quantity of electrical potential energy or else more correctly to electrical energy per time) that is provided commercially, by the electrical power industry. In a loose but common use of the term, "electricity" may be used to mean "wired for electricity" which means a working connection to an electric power station. Such a connection grants the user of "electricity" access to the electric field present in electrical wiring, and thus to electric power.

🔔 Electronics deals with electrical circuits that involve active electrical components, such as vacuum tubes, transistors, diodes and integrated circuits, and associated passive interconnection technologies.

Uses of Electricity

The present age is the age of electricity. Hence, we find various uses of electric power. The huge factories of heavy industries are easily run by electric current. The small-scale industries get into guild system and take the help of electricity. Many railway trains, trams, buses and slips are moved by electric power. X-ray photos are also taken with the help of this power. Great surgical treatments are done in the darkest nights only with the help of this powerful electric light. Machines of the radio-set, television and telescope work with the help of this power. Electric power is used in lighting the public roads, waiting rooms, conferences and meetings. The cold-storage has been possible owing to this electric power. Medical wards and cinema houses are air-conditioned only with the help of electricity. Many private persons also use this power to make their home life comfortable. Most of our articles of use are made in the factories run by the electric power. Hence, the uses of electricity are numerous.

Quick Facts

- **Electric current is measured in amperes (amps).**
- **Electric potential energy is measured in volts.**
- **Two positive charges or two negative charges repel each other, whereas, two opposite charges on the other hand attract each other.**
- **When an electric charge builds up on the surface of an object, it creates static electricity.**

- Electric eels can produce strong electric shocks of around 500 volts for both self- defence and hunting.
- Electricity travels at the speed of light – more than 186,000 miles per second!
- A spark of static electricity can measure up to 3,000 volts.
- Electric circuits can contain parts, such as switches, transformers, resistors, etc.
- Electricity can be made from wind, water, the sun and even animal poop.
- A common way to produce electricity is by hydropower, a process that generates electricity by using water to spin turbines attached to generators.
- The world's biggest source of energy for producing electricity comes from coal. The burning of coal in furnaces heats the boiler water until it becomes steam which then spins turbines attached to the generators.

Chapter - 7

CINEMA

Introduction

Cinema is the most widely acclaimed means of entertainment in the world today. It is a combination of various equipments, techniques and art which constitutes cinema.

A Zoopraxiscope

But the most important things needed to experience cinema are *camera*, *film reel* and a *projector*. **'Wheel of life'** or **'zoopraxiscope'** was the first machine to show animated pictures. It was patented in 1867 by **William Lincoln**. In a zoopraxiscope, moving photographs were watched through a slit.

The Lumière Brothers

Auguste and Louise Lumiere

"The cinema is an invention without a future." – Louis Lumière. The Lumiere brothers – **Auguste** and **Louise** - are credited for inventing the first motion picture camera in the year, **1895**. But even prior to Lumiere brothers, many others had made similar inventions. Lumiere brothers invented a *portable motion-picture camera*, film processing unit and a projector called the **Cinematographe**. Here, three functions were covered in one invention.

Lumiere's Cinematographe

Did You Know?

The first footage shot by Lumiere brothers was that of workers leaving the Lumiere factory.

Cinematographe or Cinematography brought a revolutionary change in the world of cinema and made motion pictures popular. Though, prior in 1891, the Edison Company came up with a kinetoscope which allowed to watch cinema one person at a time, Edison's vitascope (1896) was the first commercially successful projector in USA.

Edison's Vitascope

Working of Cinema

As read earlier, the cinema constitutes of equipments, techniques and art. A camera shoots an activity on a *film roll*, also known as *a film negative*. This film negative is then edited. An editor removes away unnecessary scenes by cutting away that portion of the film role. Then the edited film roll is processed in a lab with required effects.

The final film footage is then mounted on a *projector*. A projector is a device which projects the film running on the film roll on a blank white screen with the help of light.

There are *two pulleys* on a projector. The film reel is mounted on the first projector and is run through the first to the second projector with the help of a motor. The film

A Film Projector

reel passes between a magnifying lens and a light bulb. The lens increases the size of the image on the blank white screen.

Cinematography is an art form unique to *motion pictures*. Although the exposing of images on light-sensitive elements dates back to the early 19th century, motion pictures demanded a new form of photography and new aesthetic techniques. In the infancy of motion pictures, the cinematographer was usually also the director and the person physically handling the camera. As the art form and technology evolved, a separation between the director and the camera operator emerged. With the advent of artificial lighting and faster (more light sensitive) film stocks, in addition to technological advancements in optics and new techniques such as colour film and widescreen, the technical aspects of cinematography necessitated a specialist in that area.

It was a key during the silent movie era - no sound apart from background music, no dialogue - the films depended on lighting, acting and set.

In **1919**, in **Hollywood**, the *new motion picture capital of the world*, one of the first (and still existing) trade societies was formed: the *American Society of Cinematographers (ASC)*, which stood to recognise the cinematographer's contribution to the art and science of motion picture making. Similar trade associations have been established in other countries, too.

Quick Facts

- **Films are cultural artifacts created by specific cultures, which reflect those cultures, and, in turn, affect them. Film is considered to be an important art form, a source of popular entertainment and a powerful method of educating the people.**

- The visual elements of cinema give motion pictures a universal power of communication. Some films have become popular worldwide attractions by using dubbing or subtitles that translate the dialogue into the language of the viewer.

- Films are made up of a series of individual images called frames. When these images are shown rapidly in succession, a viewer has the illusion that motion is occurring. The viewer cannot see the flickering between frames due to an effect known as persistence of vision, whereby the eye retains a visual image for a fraction of a second after the source has been removed. Viewers perceive motion due to a psychological effect called the beta movement.

- CINEMA 4D is a 3D modelling, animation and rendering application developed by MAXON Computer GmbH of Friedrichsdorf, Germany. It is capable of procedural and polygonal/subd modelling, animating, lighting, texturing, rendering and common features found in 3d modelling applications.

Chapter - 8

ELECTRIC BULB

Introduction

Thomas Alva Edison is known as the inventor of the *electric bulb*. But prior to him, many other scientists had been working on manufacturing a reliable source of electric lighting.

An Electric Bulb

In **1800**, **Humphry Davy**, an *English scientist*, made the *first electric light*. He made an electric battery and to that battery, he attached a piece of carbon with a wire. When the connection was made, the piece of carbon glowed and produced light. It was called an 'electric arc'.

In **1860**, **Sir Joseph Wilson Swan**, an *English physicist*, made an *electric lamp* with a carbon paper filament. It was demonstrated in Newcastle, England. It was not a practical lamp as the filament burnt out very quickly.

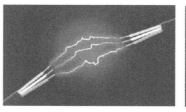

An Electric Arc

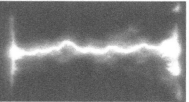

An Electric Arc between Two Metals

Thomas Alva Edison

Edison, an American inventor, experimented with hundreds of filaments before turning back to the **carbon filament**. In **1879**, he discovered that a carbon filament burns for a long time in vacuum. But it did not last longer than 40 hours. Eventually, he made a carbon filament bulb that could light for over 1500 hours.

Working of a Bulb

A bulb is a *glass sphere* with a *coiled filament* attached to the base with connecting wires. This filament has a high resistance to electric current. When the current reaches the filament, due to resistance, heat is produced. This heat becomes so much that the filament starts to glow because of it, thus, giving off light.

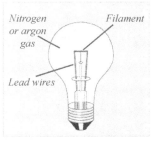

Working of A Bulb

The most difficult task before Edison was to find a filament which would:

- Have resistance and glow brightly.
- Be cheap so that bulbs could be mass produced.
- Last for a long period of time.

Did You Know?

The shape of a glass bulb was designed by **Matthew Evans** and **Henry Woodward**.

Quick Facts

- Resistance is a property of an element to oppose the flow of current. An element with high resistance towards electric current will give off high amount of heat energy.

- Incandescent bulbs are manufactured in a wide range of sizes, light output and voltage ratings, from 1.5 volts to about 300 volts. They require no external regulating equipment, have low manufacturing costs, and work equally well on either alternating current or direct current. As a result, the incandescent lamp is widely used in household and commercial lighting, for portable lighting, such as table lamps, car headlamps and flashlights, and for decorative and advertising lighting.

- An electric bulb is one of the revolutionary inventions ever made in the history of mankind. The working of an electric bulb is quite simple. When electric current flows through the filament made up of tungsten, it heats up emitting visible light.

Chapter - 9

FOUNTAIN PEN

Introduction

The first practical fountain pen was patented by **Lewis E. Waterman** in the year, **1884**. The first American patent for a pen was received by a shoemaker Peregrin Williamson in 1809. Following this, in 1819, John Scheffer received a British patent for his pen which was half quill and half metal pen.

A Fountain Pen

However, the first *self- filling fountain pen* was patented by **John Jacob Parker** in the year, **1831**. But all these fountain pens had a huge drawback – that of ink spills. This made the mass sale of these fountain pens very low.

Did You Know?

The Fountain Pen made by a Frenchman, M.Bion in the year, *1702 is the oldest pen to survive.*

A Quill Pen

The early attempts at making a pen were inspired by the working of a *feather quill.*

The first quills were made up of bird's feathers. A feather has a hollow channel through which the ink gets sucked up and get stored in it. But it is a natural object and a man-made pen on similar lines was incapable of holding the ink for long. A long, thin rubber reservoir attached to a metal nib and filled with ink was not a good option.

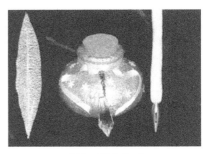

A Metal Nib Quill

Also, Lewis Waterman, who was an insurance salesman, had to cancel an important sales contact with leaky pens to start work on improving his fountain pen.

Mechanism of a Fountain Pen

A fountain pen has three parts: a nib, a feed (black part under the nib) and a barrel. The nib comes in contact with paper. The feed regulates the ink flow from the reservoir to the nib. The round barrel, holding the nib and feed on the writing end encases the ink reservoir. **Lewis Waterman** thought of adding an air hole in the nib and three grooves inside the feed.

Fountain pens have an internal reservoir of ink. Different pens had different concepts of filling the reservoirs. Earlier pens used droppers to fill ink. By **1915**, most pens were equipped by *self-filling ink reservoirs* made of rubber. The reservoirs were squeezed flat and then the nib was inserted in the ink bottle. The pressure on the reservoir was released and the nib would then suck up the ink to fill the empty reservoir.

- The fountain pen's design came after a thousand years of using quill-pens. Several different patents issued for the self-filling fountain pen design are: The Button Filler: Patented in 1905 and first offered by the Parker Pen Co. in 1913 as an alternative to the eyedropper method, it is an external button connected to the internal pressure plate that flattened the ink sac when pressed.

- The Lever Filler: Walter Sheaffer patented the lever filler in 1908. The W.A. Sheaffer Pen Company of Fort Madison, Iowa introduced it in 1912. An external lever depressed the flexible ink sac. The lever fitted flush with the barrel of the pen when it was not in use. The lever filler became the winning design for the next forty years, the button filler coming in second.

- The Click Filler: First called the crescent filler, Roy Conklin of Toledo commercially produced the first one. A later design by Parker Pen Co. used the name click filler. When two protruding tabs on the outside of the pen pressed, the ink sac deflated. The tabs would make a clicking sound when the sac was full.

- The Matchstick Filler: Introduced around 1910 by the Weidlich Company, it is a small rod mounted on the pen or a common matchstick depressed the internal pressure plate through a hole in the side of the barrel.

- The Coin Filler: Developed by Lewis Waterman in an attempt to compete with the winning lever filler patent belonging to Sheaffer, it is a slot in the barrel of the pen enabled a coin to deflate the internal pressure plate, a similar idea to the matchstick filler.

Chapter - 10

PRINTING PRESS

Introduction

The invention of printing press is the most revolutionary aspect of *modern mass communication*. The world of print communication is solely depended on the printing press.

Modern Printing Press

A printing press is a device used for inking the surface of the paper with a set pattern, usually text, by applying pressure on the paper surface.

A printing press is used to *publish books, magazines, newspapers, leaflets, brochures, posters* and other *literature*.

Johannes Gutenberg's Printing Press

The world's first printing press was set up by Johannes Gutenberg in the year **1440**. He was a *German goldsmith*, who along with **Andreas Dritzehn** and **Andreas Heilmann** started the printing press. Dritzehn was a gem cutter and Heilmann was the owner of a paper mill. With the help of his knowledge of metals, Gutenberg

started making movable metal/ wooden letters type blocks. By 1436, he had made type blocks to be used in his printing press.

Gutenberg's printing press was a hand press on which a wooden form held together the raised hand set block letters. The ink was poured over on this wooden form and this was then pressed against the sheet of paper.

Johannes Gutenberg

Did You Know?

Johannes Gutenberg printed *world's first book using movable type printing press*. It was a **42 line (42 words per page) Bible**. It is called **Gutenberg's Bible**.

Working of a Printing Press

Gutenberg's Printing Press

A printing press is made up of different sizes and types of rollers attached to it. Ink is poured over the first roller so that it spreads evenly on the whole surface and covers the area evenly. After the ink is rolled on the cylinders, the colour is transferred to the cylinder which contains the text or image plate. This roller turns in a periodic

manner at exact same rotation speed. The text/image are transferred to a blanket cylinder. A sheet of paper is inserted between this blanket cylinder and impression cylinder. All these cylinders rotate simultaneously in a similar manner to get a good print.

Quick Facts

- During the centuries, many newer printing technologies were developed based on Gutenberg's printing machine -- e.g. the offset printing.

- Gutenberg began experimenting with metal typography (Letterpress Printing) after he had moved from his native town of Mainz to Strassburg around 1430. Gutenberg concluded that metal type could be reproduced much more quickly once a single mould had been fashioned.

- The Diamond Sutra, a Buddhist scripture, was the first dated example of block printing.

- Gutenberg completed his wooden press which used movable metal type.

- The first known colour printing came out of a Psalter (a collection of Psalms for devotional use) by Faust in 1457.

- Two hundred woodcuts were used in an edition of Aesop's Fables.

- The first use of copper engravings instead of woodcuts for illustration was made in 1476.

- Printing had become established in more than 2500 cities around Europe by the year, 1499.

Chapter - 11

TELEVISION

Introduction

Television is a *medium of mass communication*. It is a device which *receives* and *transmits* moving images *(audio and video)*. Television is the most important medium of **electronic communication**.

A Modern Television

The word, television is made up of two words – Greek word, 'tele' meaning far and Latin word, 'visio' meaning sight. Thus, the word, television means 'far sight'.

John Logie Baird

The invention of *television* cannot be credited to a single person. Many people have worked towards its development. However, John Logie Baird is considered to be the person responsible for the invention of television. Prior to Baird, many inventions were made based on whom he set up his television design. **Ferdinand Braun**, in the year **1897**, invented the **cathode ray**

tube which is the most important element of a television setup. In the year 1907, the cathode ray tube was first used to produce television images.

He is credited for being the first person to produce a *live and moving greyscale image* from reflected light. In 1923-1924, he made the *world's first working television set* using things like old hatbox, scissors, sewing needles, bicycle lenses, sealing wax and glue!

Did You Know?

John Baird *survived a 1000 volt electric shock* while working on his experiment.

Baird transmitted the world's first long-distance television pictures to the Central Hotel at Glasgow Central Station in the year 1927.

He set up the Baird Television Development Company Ltd in 1928. Through this company, he made the first transatlantic television transmission, from London to New York.

An Early Television

Working of a Television

The data (audio-video) is converted into electric signal. This electric signal is then transmitted through a transmitter into the atmosphere.

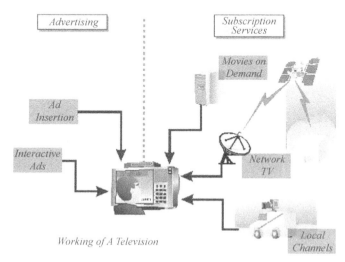

Working of A Television

These signals are then received by an antenna which converts them back into audio and video data. This data is then seen and heard on the television screen.

Philo Farnsworth

Quick Facts

- In 1938, the television broadcasts were, for the first time, able to be taped and edited. Prior to that, only live transmission was possible.

- Philo Farnsworth (Great Britain) transmitted the television image in 1927.

- In 1960 roughly 100 million television sets were sold worldwide and in 1962, the first satellite TV transmission took place between France and the United States.

- The first television transmission from the moon took place in 1969.

- In 1997, the DVD player was introduced at the Consumer Electronics Show.

- In 2005, the Flat-panel high-definition televisions became the "must have" product of the year. The Sling box product used the Internet to stream your local television anywhere in the world you've got a high speed Internet connection.

Chapter - 12

TRANSFORMER

Introduction

A transformer is an *electronic device* which is used to *transfer electric current from one circuit to another*.

A Transformer

Did You Know?

The electricity you get in your house comes to you through a *big transformer*. The *electricity board* transmits *electric current* through *wires* to a *transformer* in your residential area. This transformer then distributes the electricity to each and every house of the area. If there was no transformer, the electric current coming straight from electricity board to your house would be very high and would destroy the electric circuit in your house. Then you won't be able to run a tube light or a fan.

William Stanley

Though the *principle of induction* was discovered in as early as **1830**, William Stanley built the first advanced, commercially used transformer in the year, **1886**. However, the first transformer was invented by **Ottó**

Bláthy, Miksa Déri and **Károly Zipernowsky** of the Austro-Hungarian Empire.

His transformer was based on the basic designs by the *Ganz Company in Hungary (ZBD Transformer 1878)* and *Lucien Gaulard* and *John Dixon Gibbs in England. Gaulard and Gibbs* started the first work on transformers while Stanley made the transformer cheap to produce and easy to use.

William Stanley

Construction of a Transformer

A transformer is a device made up of an *insulated metal core* (usually iron). The two parallel arms of the iron core are coiled with copper wires. These two coils are called *primary and secondary winding*.

Working of a Transformer

The primary winding of the transformer gets the input voltage which is converted from *low voltage to high voltage or vice-versa*. To convert low voltage to high voltage, the coils in the secondary windings are increased. To convert high voltage to low voltage, the coils in the secondary windings are decreased.

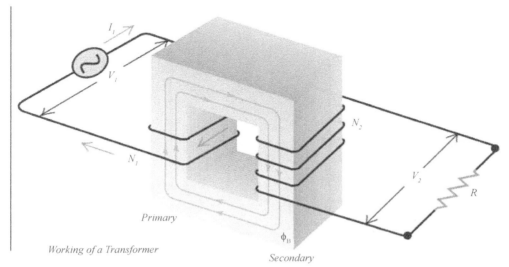

Working of a Transformer

Chapter - 13

STEAM ENGINE

Introduction

A steam engine is an engine which performs **mechanical work** using *steam* as its driving force. Though very scarcely put to use today, steam engines were a revolutionary invention and is considered as one of the greatest achievements of the modern world.

A Steam Locomotive

James Watt

Although **James Watt** is credited as the inventor of Steam Engine, *Thomas Savery* and *Thomas Newcomen* were two inventors who designed the crude and very basic steam engine.

Thomas Savery, an English military engineer, was the first to patent the basic crude steam engine in **1698**, based on the designs of *Denis Papin's pressure cooker*. Thomas Newcomen

James Watt

later improved upon Savery's design. But it was *Scotsman James Watt's* improved design which helped in ushering a new era of **Industrial Revolution**.

Did You Know?

James Watt coined the term, **'horsepower'** as a way to help explain how much work his steam engines could do for a potential buyer.

In 1765, James Watt, *a professor in the University of Glasgow*, was asked to work on improving the workability of Newcomen's designed steam engine. He attached a *separate condenser* connected to a *cylinder by a valve*. This design became very popular as it was workable and thus, James Watt is regarded as the inventor of a commercially useful steam engine.

Working of a Steam Engine

A steam engine is equipped with a *heating furnace* and a *water boiler. Coal* is used to burn the furnace and give huge amount of heat. This heat turns the water in the boiler into steam. This steam after reaching high pressure is passed through pistons and turbines. When these pistons and turbines expand, they move, and along with it moves the shaft, which at one end is attached to the wheels. This way, the heat energy is converted into mechanical energy.

Basically, a steam engine is able to *harness the energy of steam to move machinery*. It is a fairly clean source of energy. Steam engines were used to a great effect to *run locomotives and steamships*.

Quick Facts

- Industrial Revolution was the era from 1750-1850 in which many industrial reforms took place; Steam Engine is one of them.

- Steam engines are still used today to help run nuclear power plants.

- The Watt - a unit of power familiar today when dealing with lightbulbs - was named after James Watt.

- James Watt came up with the term, 'horsepower' as a way to help explain how much work his steam engines could do for a potential buyer.

- The first loco to hit 100 mph (160 km/h) was in the City of Truro in 1895.

- The Flying Scotsman was a famous loco designed by Sir Nigel Gresley (1876-1941). It pulled trains non-stop in the 630 km stretch from London to Edinhurgli in less than six hours.

- Coal and water are often stored in a wagon called a tender, towed behind the locomotive. A tender holds 10 tons of coal and 30,000 litres of water.

Chapter - 14

TELEPHONE

Introduction

The word, telephone is made up of two words, 'tele' meaning distance and 'phonetics' meaning sound. Thus, Telephone means *sound from a distance.*

A Telephone

In the beginning, there was only one kind of telephone – *a fixed cable handset with a receiver and a body with a dial pad.* It is known as **'Landline'** today. As the technology progressed, a new kind of phone came into being – **a cordless phone**.

Did You Know?

Alexander Graham Bell was the first person to invent a telephone, in the year, **1876**.

George Sweigert

George Sweigert, in **1966**, invented the *cordless phone – a portable phone without a cable.* It consisted of a handset with speaker/ receiver and a base station. This phone could be carried around within a specified range of the base station. This provided tremendous flexibility to the user. The only drawback was that it needed to be plugged into the base for charging.

Then in 1973, **Dr. Martin Cooper of Motorola** came out with the first mobile phone of the history. This is hailed as one of the *biggest revolution in the field of telecommunication*. Today, almost every person carries a **mobile phone**.

Alexander Graham Bell

He made *his first telephone* on **June 2, 1875** and at the age of 29, Bell presented his first 'telephone' to the world in the year, 1876. In 1877, he formed the **Bell Telephone Company**. Throughout his life, Bell worked for the betterment of the *deaf and mute people*. His mother lost her hearing ability later in life. This led Bell to research and invent various means of communication for such people. This interest led him to invent the **'microphone'** which formed the basis for his **'electrical speech machine'**. This machine was what we know today as telephone.

By 1878, Bell had set up the *first telephone exchange* in New *Haven, Connecticut*. By 1884, long distance connections were made between Boston, Massachusetts and New York City.

Working Components of a Telephone

As it has since its early years, the telephone instrument is made up of the following functional components: a power source, a switch hook, a dialler, a ringer a transmitter, a receiver, and an anti-sidetone circuit.

In the first experimental telephones, the electric current that powered the telephone circuit was generated at the transmitter, by means of an electromagnet activated by the speaker's voice. Such a system could not generate enough voltage to produce audible speech. So every transmitter since Bell's patented design has operated on a direct current supplied by an independent power source. The first sources were batteries located in the telephone instruments themselves, but since the 1890s, current has been generated at the local switching office. The current is supplied through a two-wire circuit called the local loop. The standard voltage is 48 volts.

Switch Hook

The switch hook connects the telephone instrument to the direct current supplied through the local loop. In early telephones, the receiver was hung on a hook that operated the switch by opening and closing a metal contact. This system is still common, though the hook has been replaced by a cradle to hold the combined handset, enclosing both the receiver and the transmitter. In some modern electronic instruments, the mechanical operation of metal contacts has been replaced by a system of transistor relays.

When the telephone is "on hook," contact with the local loop is broken. When it is "off hook" (i.e., when the handset is lifted from the cradle), contact is restored, and current flows through the loop. The switching office signals restoration of contact by transmitting a low-frequency "dial tone"—actually two simultaneous tones of 350 and 440 Hertz.

Dialler

The dialler is used to enter the number of the party that the user wishes to call. Signals generated by the dialer activate switches in the local office, which establish a transmission path to the called party. Dialers are of the rotary and push-button types.

The traditional rotary dialler, invented in the 1890s, is rotated against the tension of a spring and then released, whereupon it returns to its position at a rate controlled by a mechanical governor. The return rotation causes a switch to open and close, producing interruptions, or pulses, in the flow of direct current to the switching office. Each pulse lasts approximately one-tenth of a second; the number of pulses signals the number being dialled.

In push-button dialling, introduced in the 1960s, the pressing of each button generates a "dual-tone" signal that is specific to the number being entered. Each dual tone is composed of a low frequency (697, 770, 852, or 941 hertz) and a high frequency (1,209, 1,336, or 1,477 hertz), which are sensed and decoded at the switching office. Unlike the low-frequency rotary pulses, dual tones can travel through the telephone system, so that push-button telephones can be used to activate automated functions at the other end of the line.

In both rotary and push-button systems, a capacitor and resistor prevent dialling signals from passing into the ringer circuit.

Ringer

The ringer alerts the user to an incoming call by emitting an audible tone or ring. Ringers are of two types, mechanical or electronic. Both types are activated by a 20-hertz, 75-volt alternating current generated by the switching office. The ringer is

activated in two-second pulses, each pulse separated by a pause of four seconds.

The traditional mechanical ringer was introduced with the early Bell telephones. It consists of two closely spaced bells, a metal clapper, and a magnet. Passage of alternating current through a coil of wire produces alternations in the magnetic attraction exerted on the clapper, so that it vibrates rapidly and loudly against the bells. Volume can be muted by a switch that places a mechanical damper against the bells.

In modern electronic ringers, introduced in the 1980s, the ringer current is passed through an oscillator, which adjusts the current to the precise frequency required to activate a piezoelectric transducer—a device made of a crystalline material that vibrates in response to an electric current. The transducer may be coupled to a small loudspeaker, which can be adjusted for volume.

The ringer circuit remains connected to the local loop even when the telephone is on hook. A larger voltage is necessary to activate the ringer. A capacitor prevents direct current from passing through the ringer once the handset has been lifted off the switch hook.

Transmitter

The transmitter is essentially a tiny microphone located in the mouthpiece of the telephone's handset. It converts the vibrations of the speaker's voice into variations in the direct current flowing through the set from the power source.

In modern electric transmitters, developed in the 1970s, the carbon layer is replaced by a thin plastic sheet that has been given a conductive metallic coating on one side. The plastic separates that coating from another metal electrode and maintains an electric field between them. Vibrations caused

by speech produce fluctuations in the electric field, which in turn produce small variations in voltage. The voltages are amplified for transmission over the telephone line.

Receiver

The receiver is located in the earpiece of the telephone's handset. Operating on electromagnetic principles that were known in Bell's day, it converts fluctuating *electric current into sound waves that reproduce human speech*. Fundamentally, it consists of two parts: a permanent magnet, having pole pieces wound with coils of insulated fine wire, and a diaphragm driven by magnetic material that is supported near the pole pieces.

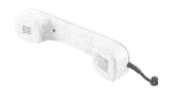

Anti-sidetone Circuit

The anti-sidetone circuit is an assemblage of *transformers, resistors, and capacitors* that perform a number of functions. The primary function is to reduce the sidetone, which is the distracting sound of the speaker's own voice coming through the receiver from the transmitter.

The *anti-sidetone circuit* accomplishes this reduction by interposing a transformer between the transmitter circuit and the receiver circuit and by splitting the transmitter signals along two paths. When the divided signals, having opposite polarities, meet at the transformer, they almost entirely cancel each other in crossing to the receiver circuit. The speech signal coming from the other end of the line, on the other hand, arrives at the transformer along a single, undivided path and crosses the transformer undisturbed.

Working of a Telephone

A telephone consists of a microphone which converts the sound waves into electric current and sends it through a telephone network to another phone. The earphone or speaker in the receiving phone converts this electric signal back into sound wave.

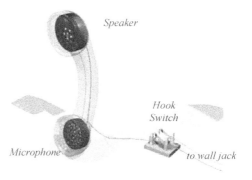

Working of a Telephone

Quick Facts

- The telephone network extends worldwide, so you can reach nearly anyone on the planet.

- Alexander Graham Bell experimented with his "harmonic telegraph" for two years before getting patented by the U.S. Patent Office. On March 10, 1876 he was able to get his phone to work.

- The first words spoken through a telephone were "Watson come here, I want you!" The phone call was made by Alexander Graham Bell to his assistant, Thomas A. Watson.

- Mark Twain was one of the first people to have a phone in his home.

- Alexander Graham Bell also invented the metal detector.

- When Alexander Graham Bell died in 1922, all telephones stopped from ringing for one full minute as a tribute to the creator.

- The first transatlantic telephone cable was used in 1956. A telephone cable was run across the ocean floor and lies as deep as 12,000 feet. The cable runs across the Atlantic Ocean from Canada to Scotland.

Chapter - 15

ELECTRIC MOTOR

Introduction

An electric motor is a device which turns or converts *electrical energy* into *mechanical energy*.

An Electric Motor

Electric motors are found in many appliances, ranging from small devices like electric wrist watch, pump, geyser, blower, mixer-juicer, to bigger appliances like fans, air conditioners, coolers, industrial mills, etc.

Electric motors of high efficiency were started being made from 1821. However, the first commercially successful motor was made in 1873. The working of an electric motor is based on **Faraday's law of induction**.

Nikola Tesla

Nikola Tesla made the first **Alternating Current** or **AC Motor** in the year, 1888. AC or Alternate Current Motor was an admirable step towards highly efficient and less heat generating motor advancement. Prior to that, in the year **1886**, **Frank Julian Sprague** had made a DC or Direct Current Motor. The AC motors had an advantage over DC motors as the former provided high efficiency and could run most of the appliances without conversion.

Today, only Alternating Current or AC motors are mostly used because AC is the general form in which electricity is carried to homes, offices, businesses, industries, etc.

Working of an Electric Motor

A simple motor consists of the following six parts – *rotor, commutator, brushes, axle, field magnet* and *power supply*.

The field magnet is a **permanent magnet**. The **wire coil** is wrapped around an **armature**. The wire coil is attached to a source of current. When the electric current flows through the wire coil, a **magnetic field** develops around the armature. Thus, the armature behaves like an **electromagnet**. Now the field

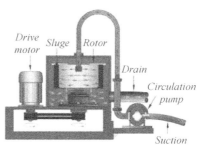

Working of a Electric Motor

magnet attracts and repels the magnetised armature. This makes the armature move a full rotation. This armature is attached with a shaft at one end with the help of an axle. When the axle moves because of repeated rotation of the armature, mechanical energy is produced. Thus, the *electrical energy* is converted into *mechanical energy*.

- Michael Faraday's law of induction states the relationship between the production of mechanical force by the interaction of electric current and magnetic field.

- Most electric motors operate through the interaction of magnetic fields and current-carrying conductors to generate force.

- Electric motors and generators are commonly referred to as electric machines.

- They may be powered by direct current, e.g., a battery powered portable device or motor vehicle, or by alternating current from a central electrical distribution grid or inverter.

- The smallest motors may be found in electric wristwatches.

Glossary

Astronomer: A scientific observer of celestial bodies

Philosopher: A person who is deeply versed in philosophy

Inclination: Bent, a disposition

Premature: Immature, mature or ripe before proper time

Maternal: Related through mother

Enrolled: Enlisted, to put in record

Electrolysis: The conduction of electricity by a solution

Knighted: A man upon whom the non-hereditary dignity of knighthood (honour)

Experiences: Process or act of personally encountering

Wonder: To think or speculate curiously

Proposed: To suggest, offer

Accurate: Exact, precise

Microbiologist: A branch of Biology dealing with the structure and function of micro-organisms

Rabies: An infectious disease of dogs or cats transmitted by bite to human beings

Anthrax: An infectious, often fatal disease of cattle, sheep, etc.

Souring: Having an acid taste, fermented

Sanitize: Sterilize, make free from dirt, germs, etc.

Gadgets: Mechanical devices

Immune: Protected or exempted from a disease

Prestigious: Honourable, having a high reputation

Sterilization: Disinfected, making germ-free

Superseded: To succeed to the position in power

Exploration: Investigation

Properties: Qualities, features

Emitted: Discharged, reflected

Eradicate: To remove or destroy completely

Tumour: A swollen part, protuberance

Unaware: Not aware or conscious, unconscious

Supplement: Something added to complete a thing

Phonograph: Any sound-reproducing-machine

Filament: A very fine threadlike structure

Incandescent: Glowing or white with heat, brilliant

Complications: Confusions, a complex combination of events

Inspiration: A divine influence

Perspiration: Sweating, the act of eliminating fluid through the pores of the skin

Intellectual: A person of superior intelligence

Attainments: Accomplishments, Achievements

Pivotal: Vital, very important

Evolve: Develop gradually

Eminent: Prominent, noteworthy, distinguished, reputed

Immense: Vast, huge, very great

Variations: Amount, rate, extent or degree of change

Stagnated: Still and become stale

Amidst: Within, surrounding

Harsh: Unpleasant, ungentle

STUDENT DEVELOPMENT/LEARNING
(छात्र विकास/लर्निंग)

JOKES
(हास्य)

 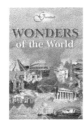   

   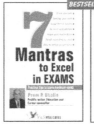 

 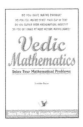   

MAGIC & FACT (जादू एवं तथ्य)

MUSIC (संगीत)

COMPUTER

All books available at **www.vspublishers.com**

Quiz Books
(प्रश्नोत्तरी की पुस्तकें)

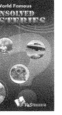

MYSTERIES
(रहस्य)

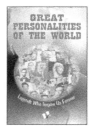
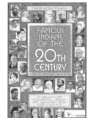

DRAWING BOOKS (ड्राइंग बुक्स)

BIOGRAPHIES (आत्म कथाएँ)

QUOTES/SAYINGS (उद्धरण/सूक्तिवाणी)

PUZZLES (पहेलियाँ)

ACTIVITIES BOOK (एक्टिविटीज बुक)

Contact us at sales@vspublishers.com

CHILDREN'S ENCYCLOPEDIA
(बच्चों के ज्ञानकोश)

CHILDREN'S ENCYCLOPEDIA
THE WORLD OF KNOWLEDGE

All Books in Full Colour

Free CD for additional reference

Set of 5 Books In Attractive Gift Box

Code: 02152 S

LIFE SCIENCES and HUMAN BODY

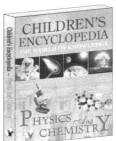

PHYSICS and CHEMISTRY

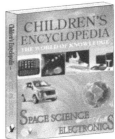

SPACE SCIENCE and ELECTRONICS

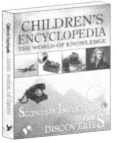

SCIENTISTS INVENTIONS and DISCOVERIES

GENERAL KNOWLEDGE

---

71 SERIES (71 श्रृंखला)

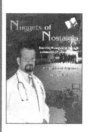